# For A Little While

AMY LAURENS

## OTHER WORKS

Find other works by the author at
http://www.amylaurens.com/books/

# For A Little While

AMY LAURENS

Australia

Copyright © 2018 Amy Laurens
2 4 6 8 10 9 7 5 3 1

All rights reserved. No part of this book may be reproduced in any form or by any electronic or mechanical means, including information storage and retrieval systems, without permission in writing from the publisher, except by a reviewer, who may quote brief passages in a review.

This is a work of fiction. All characters, organisations and events are the author's creation, or are used fictitiously.

ISBN: 978-1-925825-84-8

www.inkprintpress.com

*National Library of Australia Cataloguing-in-Publication Data*
Laurens, Amy 1985 –
For A Little While
84p.    cm.
ISBN: 978-1-925825-84-8
Inkprint Press, Canberra, Australia
1. Poetry—Women Authors 2. Australian Poetry—Women Authors 3. Families—Poetry 4. Social Problems—Poetry

Summary: Ranging from the quiet ache of mundane drudgery to the deep, searing pain of injustice and world tragedies, this collection of poems by Amy Laurens offer quiet hope for the world-weary soul.

First Edition: July 2018
Printed in Australia.

Cover design © Amy Laurens
Cover photo © Aaron Burden via Unsplash

## *CONTENTS*

| | |
|---|---|
| In The Evening, Where The Deserts End | 8 |
| No One Ever Said | 10 |
| Observations of an Evergreen | 12 |
| Your Scratched-Out Nails Are Beautiful | 13 |
| On Weekdays | 14 |
| Plane Travel | 16 |
| One | 18 |
| Weaving Magic | 20 |
| Ducks in Stormy Weather | 21 |
| Poetry of a Scientist at Heart | 22 |
| Seasickness | 24 |
| When You Are Asleep | 25 |
| Float | 26 |
| A Conversation | 28 |
| Portrait of You, Aged Two | 30 |
| Dawn Landing | 32 |
| Let Us Be Explorers | 34 |
| Before I Speak | 36 |
| Priests of The Sandringham Line | 37 |
| At The Shrine of the Godless | 38 |
| Anxiety I | 40 |
| Wisdom Is a River (Not a Storm) | 43 |
| A Letter to Blue | 44 |
| Anxiety II | 46 |
| Not Black, A Woman | 48 |

| | |
|---|---|
| Australian Land | 51 |
| One Way or Another | 52 |
| There Are Days | 54 |
| Writing : Life | 57 |
| Saving Me | 58 |
| When We Know Better | 62 |
| Nothing Is Enough | 64 |
| Weltschmerz | 66 |
| What Do I Want You to Know? | 68 |
| Recipe for My Daughter | 70 |
| Here Is My Body | 72 |
| Recipe for My Son | 74 |
| Stand Up | 76 |
| Liminal Spaces | 77 |
| Remember | 80 |

*About The Author*

## *IN THE EVENING, WHERE THE DESERTS END*

In the evening, when my heart
is as full as the sky is of stars,
then I will go out to the dunes of
sand that stretch endlessly to the sea, and
there I will wait.
In the sparkling
starlight of the night, I will wait
for you,
and when you come we will leap
hand in hand
down slopes that fall away under our feet until
we can fly,
and together we will soar
through the night like bats,
great, leathery wings of belief
pinning us to the sky.
We will dip and twist and glide and turn, and
when we have flown high enough, your hand clenched
tightly in mine like we are locked together eternally,
we will reach the stars.

The dunes will stretch below like a sea,
waves of sand frozen in place only
by time and perspective, and
we will see that the boundaries of our desert
are finite;
that the barrenness of our minds comes to
an end;
and that outside it all is fertile.
Together
we will swoop back to the ground and remember
what we have seen from our vantage
point of the stars: we will walk onwards
with steps that achingly climb, only to slip
back halfway to where they came from, and
our muscles will burn
as we scale the heights of our
disappointments
—but we will not forget.
We have been to the stars,
and they have shown us:
the desert too will
end.

One day, we will find the fence, and scale it.

## *NO ONE EVER SAID*

No one ever said:
You must love only perfect things.
So when I tell you,
"I love my body."
I'm not claiming perfection,
or delusion,
or illusion.
It's unfit, like a jellyfish with bones;
it's neglected, a latch-key kid in its own skin;
it's flabs-not-abs,
scars-not-spas,
pores-not-cores.

You are telekinetic.
Did you know that?
(Telekinesis is moving things
purely by the power of thought;
how else do you move your fingers
when you type?)

My body walks
my body runs
my body hugs and breathes and eats,
feels fresh air upon my cheeks and
rain upon my hair and
sun upon my arms and
the soft, damp kisses of my child upon my nose and
the warm, strong embrace of my husband 'round my waist and
the careful shoulder knocks,
fists bumps,
high-fives
from students who want to connect.

My body made a baby.
My body made a baby with zero
conscious effort on my part.
That's *better* than telekinesis.
That's magic.

Your body is like magic.
Did you know that?
And love isn't only for the perfect.

## *OBSERVATIONS OF AN EVERGREEN*

In any daily weather
without design
or desultory portent
they let fall
leaves of fire and gold.

Naked they stand
illuminated
by sun,
showers,
age.

In time
new buds will come
But for now they face
the ravages of winter
naked
stripped bare.

To let leaves fall
requires courage
more than I have.

## *YOUR SCRATCHED-OUT NAILS ARE BEAUTIFUL*

Truly, your bitten-nail fingers, covered
with scratched-out polish and messy cuticles and
love and
stress and
worry
are the most beautiful thing about you.
When I look at them, I see:
        you know
        you feel
        you care.
Beneath the ragged crust of keratin
designed to protect your nerves from harm
are the parts of you that feel most deeply,
need most keenly,
share most openly
            And these,
your ragged nails, your scratched-out attempts
at conforming to society's expectations—
        they are just a cover.
These nails, they show
you for what you truly are
and you are beautiful,
because you care.

## *ON WEEKDAYS*

On weekdays, I
board the bus or
ride the train
just one in a shifting sea of thousands
washing up against the shore of necessity
working to provide
food
clothes
shelter
toys

In every vehicle
on every road and track
we sleep
eyes closed against the harsh realities of morning
sun blinding-bright,
dew-soaked and new

Headphones,
to block thought
Sunglasses,
to hide away souls
Windows, to tint away
the poverty of the streets,
poor in
food
clothes
shelter
respect

The sun is bright in the morning.
It hurts sometimes to see.

## *PLANE TRAVEL*

You　　　　　　　　start
like　　　　　　　　this

    elbows in
  ankles crossed
 never touching

    but   s  l  o  w  l  y

you start to s
            p
              r
                a
                    w
                        l

Because    HOUR  HOUR  HOUR
                 HOUR  HOUR  HOUR
                 HOUR  HOUR  HOUR
                 HOUR  HOUR  HOUR
                 HOUR  HOUR

                        is a really long time.

      Elbows bump.
      (sorry)
      Knees touch.
       Sorry.
A baby's foot brushes your leg.
        Sorry!
It's not a problem. Also, he's adorable.
       …Thanks!

This is how friendships begin.

Is fourteen hours long enough to make
               a friend?

     Maybe.
   in the right time
   in the right place
with the right people.

     Either way,

    You   can
   now sit
        likethis.

## *ONE*

I kiss your velvet head and
your body warms my lips, as mine
did yours, and I wonder
what is the meaning of this?
I gaze into your dark grey eyes,
bright lacquer in a matt-finish face, gleaming
precious jewels that speak
in peach-petal skin;
why is this important?

You cram your fist into your mouth,
like an aggrandising teen,
but you are tiny, and
you have nothing to prove, and I
always have something to prove.

I cradle you and you are my body's negative space
There is you and
There is me and
we fit.

You smile because you are standing and that
is a feat of mechanics, defying gravity so
I wish that I could smile more because I stand
laugh more because I breathe
cram my fingers into my mouth because I can.

And that is the secret, the meaning:
I have grown old
I know that you are not me
that you are Other
that I am Other;
You know that we are One.

## *WEAVING MAGIC*

As you tangle fingers in my untamed hair
lips meet, and
tongues touch, and
you are the sweetness of someone without guile.
Running fingers down my thigh, soft,
like a bird, you weave
magic to make me beautiful, blessing
stretch-marked places,
cellulit places,
not-so-perfectly-tanned places,
places society is ashamed of.
You call me lovely, and I press against
the nakedness of your words,
the brush of your chocolate forelock,
the whisper of rough stubble across my cheek,
the ghost of your hand in mine;
I am beautiful.

## *DUCKS IN STORMY WEATHER*

Ducks, like beached boats
In rows on the river banks

Lie beneath the howling wind
Like hulls disused in winter's grip

Feathers ruffled by the tempest,
Like peeling paint attacked by elements

Wind, which sometimes skims
Ducks under swollen clouds

Or lets them cut across the breasts
Of waves, wings full of air, as sails,

Now forces ducks aground
To wait for kinder weather.

## *POETRY OF A SCIENTIST AT HEART*

'Flagellated protozoan'
Is the best rhyme I can find
For 'trying to write a poem'
How amusing

'Flagellated protozoan'
Seems to mean 'a little creature
That is never found in poem'—
How confusing

And it isn't really rhyming
And the rhythm is all out
A stupendous lack of timing
Shows throughout it

And the harder that I ponder
And the longer that I try
The worse the poem wanders
All about

So I'm stuck here with a poem
About whip-like protozoans
And I think that I'm not meant
To be a poet

So I'll put away thesauri
And I'll go back to my lab
And I'll play with
protozoans: flagellated
instead.

## *SEASICKNESS*

The smell of defrosting prawns
baking in the sunlight
The taste of salt and vinegar
chips, eaten from a packet
shared with fishy hands

The movement of the boat
wallowing in the water like
a pregnant sea cow
The sloshing of stomach,
guts, brain
The gently insistent attack
of the wind
knotting hair, salt-coating
skin, clothes, eyes
until you are sticky

Seasickness, like madness, drifts
on the wind, coming
in waves, with the waves.

## *WHEN YOU ARE ASLEEP*

I scoop you up in my arms and
press my cheek against your hair and
it is soft and thick
like feathers,
or more accurately,
like Labradog fur,
which is an odd comparison until
you remember how much I miss my dog.
I am carrying you wrong,
shoulders stooped,
back hunched,
but there is no wrong way to carry someone
when they will only fit into your arms
for a little while.

## *FLOAT*

Books cannot hold
my attention when I'm
restless, tired,
guilty.

*(How dare I read, when this is my house:*
*Toys and discarded food scraps in the corner and*
*misshapen folding like an awkward visitor on the lounge and*
*paperwork as unfinished as the days of summer on the table and*
*dishes stacked on the bench like so many used goods.*
*Wet laundry skulks in the corner, waiting*
*to be hung*
*like flags,*
*bunting made of our second skins,*
*Small Person's caterpillar suit and*
*my favourite shirt I should have thrown out months ago and*
*sheets my husband and I bought together*
*lie in together*
*change together;*
*these sheets have seen so*
*much of our marriage.)*

Guilt sours the taste of cherries,
because cherries are expensive
and out of season.

*(People die for want
of food, and you dare
ship yours in
from America?)*

When I am drowning in a sea
of liquid guilt, it is tempting
to sink down.
Guilt is heavy, after all.
But when I am drowning
in a sea of liquid guilt,
sometimes I remember
that my body
can also float, if I just lie
still.

## *A CONVERSATION*

The set:
A moving vehicle
ten over eighty
on a sunbright morning
a steel grey afternoon
a shining, shimmering night.

The cast:
A husband, thirty-five;
competent driver.
A son, three and five
weeks, back seat critic.
And me. Observer.
Recorder.

The script:
"Go faster, Daddy! Go faster!"
Ten, we recall, over eighty.
"Can't, son. The policeman
would tell me off."
A pause. Consideration.
"The policeman would tell you to stop?"
"Yes, son, he would. And
if a policeman tells you to stop,
what do you do?"
"You stop, Daddy."
"You do. The policemen are there
to help you."

The observation:
My heart
crumpling in my chest
crushed because
my son is white.
For him,
the policemen will always help.

## *PORTRAIT OF YOU, AGED TWO*

Golden ponytail and
chubby-cheeked grin,
you are a slip of light
in the shadows of our dusty house
you take up all the room,
or else, no room at all,
depending on your mood,
the weather,
the time of day,
the direction the wind is blowing.
'Nicorns and bunnies line your
room, your
clothes, your
smile, soft and velvety and delightful
and sharp-pointed, like a unicorn's horn;
This is you:
giggles, "I'm happy", shrieking with delight,
sharp-pointed stubborn determination.
Your brother cannot wear you down.

In the wardrobe, a poster, made for you at birth:
Let her sleep, for when she wakes, she
will move mountains.
At two, you already move the mountains
of our affection
the mountains of our
attention,
and we tumble, cartwheeling around you
never giving in to your gravity for good, to
crash and burn against the shores
of whims and tantrums, but
never happy to see you sad,
because although your snuggles
soothe my heart like aloe, your
tears can drown a room.
You are golden, like the sun, and just as fierce;
within you burns a fire that one day,
all the world will stand before in awe
and tremble, as you move
the mountains of their lives as well.

## *DAWN LANDING*

Oh, conveyor belt of traffic, moving
like ants down your predetermined path
blinkered from the magic of the world.
Beyond you, fog flows
like literal rivers down
from the mountains to pool
like glacial lakes in valleys,
ripples carved by the wind, a
white-foam river frozen
in time
while waterfalls tumble down cliffs
Perpetually—
or at least until the sun rises.

Oh, traffic, on your daily belt
that moves inexorably from
home
to work
to home
for you there is no horizon
save the city skyline.

Up here
there is no horizon at all
or if there is, it's way beyond the clouds,
sea fading seamlessly into sky below
with a banner of puff-nosed cottonballs,
and waves curling to foam at the toes of
bite-shaped cliffs,
the sunrise reflected on a blurred propeller, that
fantasy which keeps our plane in flight,
the only indication of its quick existence
a smear of pink.

The thud of landing that jolts magic
from the world;
The return to city noise,
grating, prosaic.

## *LET US BE EXPLORERS*

Let us
>hold hands together and head
>to places we have not been in forever
>that exist only in distant memories
>of having-been-their-once,
>of having-seen-that-then

Together, let us
>feast upon the honey that falls fresh from combs,

and
>travel south, to the springtime of
>the awakening bud, and then
>the strong branch that, laden,
>drips with new-pressed wine

Then let us
>climb the mountains of myrrh, and
>feast on pomegranates in the secret garden
>gently peel them open to suck
>at flesh pink, and pure, and delicious

Afterwards, let us stand
        before the tower of David
        run fingers over satin sides of silk
        caress the fawns that hide among the lilies, and
        kiss the small pink seashells of our shores

Let us do these things
and let us do them slowly
for we are explorers
in no rush for anything
but the journey.

## *BEFORE I SPEAK*

I have spilled
words onto the page
like sugar granules or
high fructose corn syrup
just because I could

but now
is the hour to be silent.

Very soon
I will speak words
like rain
in torrents
life in a parched throat
each drop sweet and
wholesome and
crystal, crystal clear

but now
is the hour to be silent
to let moisture gather
on my dust
before I speak.

be silent / gather / speak.

## *PRIESTS OF THE SANDRINGHAM LINE*

They enter under vow of silence,
dressed in black
business suits and skirts and
I am out of place,
in my jeans
and polar-fleece hoodie
and green canvas bag.
Yet together, we join in silent prayer,
heads bowed to the god
of finance, who drives us
by necessity
from our sleep at this early hour.
They sway and dance
and the woman's sequin-beaded
handbag with the stylised strawberry
glitters like an offering, a sacrifice
bought to please an ever-hungry deity.
The carriage stops;
priests scatter to their houses
of worship, and are replaced,
and the carriage clacks
onwards, carrying priests
of the Sandringham line.

## *AT THE SHRINE OF THE GODLESS*

Deep in the woods
where the light filters down,
and the godless kneel
with their heads to the ground,
not a creature stirs and
the wind is still
as it pauses to hear
a dead man's will.

For this is the shrine
of murderers, knaves;
people whose fingers
outnumber their days.
This is the place
where the scoundrels go
before they are tied
in a hangman's bow.

For here, if they cry
there's a chance they'll be heard
by the creature who's bound
by iron and word—
and if they are lucky, and
if they are blessed,
the darkness won't hear and
their death will mean rest.

But if they are cursed
and their mutterings true,
they'll waken the demon
whom God never knew.
They'll take their place
in the deathcap row,
spirits entrapped here
forever ago

by the violence and evil that
sooted their hearts,
withered their conscience,
corrupted their arts.
Yet still they will kneel,
though they hear the cries
of the dead men before them
who clung to their lives,

for this is the place
where the dead men grow,
this is the shrine
of the godless.

## *ANXIETY I*

The best way to fight a lion
is to not.
Instead,
approach it sideways,
from the very edges,
looking vague, and non-threatening.
When it realises you are there—
and it will—
it will growl, and bear
its teeth, which feels
a lot like a lump in your throat
or adrenalin in your stomach.
But you would do the same
if you were afraid.
So keep circling it,
a nice distance away,
smiling and nodding, and looking reassuring.
Soothe the poor lion,
who is disturbed by your gaze,
and slowly, slowly,
it will let you closer.

The only way to pat a lion
is carefully.
Tangle your fingers through its mane,
whisper to it that everything will be alright.
and when it bares its teeth
and flashes its claws,
stand ready, alert (but never alarmed;
most people do not die by lion),
jump out of the way if you need to—
but make sure you always return.
Your lion needs you.

Hold your lion.
Cradle its massive head in your lap,
admire the way it looks,
so strong, so powerful.
It only desires to protect you.
Croon to it.
Promise it the world.
Remind it that although you do not have
teeth, or claws,
you have other weapons, stronger:
Logic. Planning. Forethought.
These are the kind of weapons
that protect you from harm
before it even finds you.
(Lions are not logic. Lions do not plan.
Never mistake their murmurings
for logic, or forethought, or plans.)

No one *needs* a lion.
But once you have one,
It is very hard
to let it go.
So the best you can do is hold it.
Feed it gently,
treat it kindly,
reassure it
(as you would yourself, if you were scared)
and it will love you well.
But do always remember:
It's not a *tame* lion.

## *WISDOM IS A RIVER (NOT A STORM)*

Wisdom doesn't come
in an hour.
And although we long
for grand epiphanies
to light the way through our lives,
it is never the last step that matters,
but the next one;
only ever the next one.

It would be nice, one imagines,
to plug one's cortex in,
Matrix-style,
and learn things easily,
quickly.
But wisdom doesn't come
in an hour.
And although storms may savage the world
and cause great upheaval,
the change that lasts the longest is the river,
slowly carving its banks
until one day, it lies in a gorge
beneath the plateau
and the landscape all around
is changed for good.

## *A LETTER TO BLUE*

Yes, okay, I'm feeling blue.
It's kind of a light summery aqua, not a navy, so it's easier,
but it's like:
Okay,
there is blue.
This does not actually change anything.
Yay blue.
Hi blue.
Blue is fine.
Blue is not in charge,
Red is not in charge,
Purple is not in charge.
Blue is not in charge not because it's blue,
but because it's a feeling, and
feelings don't get to be in charge.

They get to help
(lots)
they get to advise
(lots)
but they only get to be in charge when I decide they are in charge
and right now, nope, not in charge.

So.
Yes, I see you blue
you are there, and you are blue,
and you can go and sit in your little blue corner and be blue,
and that is fine.
But while you do that, I'm just going to be over here,
being competent,
and you can join me when you're done.
Okay?

## *ANXIETY II*

In good times,
it is possible for a lion
to purr.
(If you have not seen this,
you will not believe me.)
Your lion wants to keep you safe.
Because of this,
occasionally,
when you *are* safe
and your lion sees this,
it will rub its cheeks against you
and purr, like the distant rumble
of thunder on the horizon.
Your lion loves you.
Your lion lives to make you proud.

Of course,
there are times when
you are perfectly safe
and all your lion wants to do is grumble—
a snarling pulse, flash-clawed adrenalin in your chest—
but that doesn't make the purring
any softer
when it comes;
purring is just as valid whether it is
part of a continual stream,
or bookended by growling and complaints.
And lions, after all, are lions.
They will do both depending on their whims.

## *NOT BLACK, A WOMAN*

I am not black,
and if you know anything about the world at all, you know

that that means more terrible
things than the physical
chemistry of my skin,
more than what kind of places
I can blend in;
it means I'm a societal circle
confronted
by circular societal holes;
it means I'll never know what it's like
to reach for my wallet just a little too fast
and be confronted
by circular holes
in my skin.

I'm not black.
But I am a woman.
and although at first the two
might seem so
yawn
        ingly

different

they don't even relate as opposites:

listen.

I am a woman. I know
what it's like to know
that every move you make
can be interpreted
in a hundred
thousand
million
billion
trillion
ways more than you intended.

I know what it's like to stand
military-stiff with alertness as
the possibilities
of the game flash
through your mind:
If I do this, will they think that?
If I do that, will they think this?
If I
move my arm, if I
flick my hair, if I
shift my weight, if I
smile, if I
frown, if I
meet their gaze, if I
ignore their eyes, if I
put my head up head down shoulders straight shoulders round...

Girls read body language well, not
because we're wired differently, but
because it can be a matter of life and death.
Black boys
read body language well, not
because they're guilty,
but because
it's a matter of life and death.

## *AUSTRALIAN LAND*

It is a funny thing,
to own land, and yet
not own it.
I never paid for that hill,
the one I consider mine,
and no deed to it ever bore my name;
and yet, when I look upon it
now
and see the devastation that's
been wrought,
I want to rip the land away from them
before I vomit;
People who can gouge such
wanton scars into the land
do not deserve to own it.

(And then, of course, I wonder
what it must be like
to have been feeling this
since April 1770.)

## *ONE WAY OR ANOTHER*

I too was raised until the banner of bigger is better.
It wasn't deliberate, I'm sure
Symptomatic, not designed
A systemic, self-imposed logic
(of sorts):
Bigger *must* be better, because
what can small do to help
in a world such as ours?

But sometimes,
even 'big' isn't big enough.

Sometimes even 'big'
isn't big enough if
what you're trying to be
is the whole solution.

When you are raised on 'bigger is better',
it's often impossible to
not be the whole of the solution.
Logic dictates
that every drop
will help to wear away the stone,
but to our hearts it feels trite,
and small.
And what can small do
in a world such as ours?

But here is a secret: the small
Bore lets in the great auger.

Here is another secret:
We are not here
to fix the world.

I long for justice;
I ache for mercy.
And every act I make
works either in their favour,
or against.

Everything tips the balance
One way or another.

## *THERE ARE DAYS*

There are days
when the world sucks
at your feet,
when every step is a long
schhhhhhhllurPOP
of effort, as you grind
against the forces that hold you down.
Depression isn't a fight, it's a slog.

There are days when everything you feel
is caked with mud
and the mud isn't yellow, or
white, or brown;
It's grey, just
grey
and it fills your eyes, your soul.

(For me, sleep is restorative
at least if I do it right
which I hardly ever seem to these days;
I'm sleep-challenged,
dysleepsic.
Oh, how I wish I could sleep.)

There are days
when all we can do is trudge onward,
onward,
onward,
trusting in the journey,
stretching out a hand to those who
trudge along our sides—
to help, or be helped;
there are days when you cannot tell
these things apart
(but you stretch out your hand regardless, hoping
that someone will catch you
and pull you on)

There are days
when the only sound outside
the constant clamour of my heart,
telling me to stop
to just lie down—
is your voice.
You.
Your hand.

Your hand looks different every time.
There are days when it looks like
puppies, frolicking in my feed,
or blessings, prayed through my inbox,
or just a simple hug
or a smile.
Either way, your hand is there.

Some days, it's your hand that keeps me going.
Not fighting,
it's not a fight.
Fights are active.
Fights are purposeful.
But I do keep going. Every day.

## *WRITING : LIFE*

A thought on writing:
Anything I love will hurt;
might as well be this.

A thought on life:
Anything I love will hurt;
might as well be this.

## *SAVING ME*

I am late to the party, because
I always am
what with one thing or another, but
here I am at last,
and I bear cake.

I
What is saving me is this:
wonderful blogs,
space of my own to
say what I'm thinking
think what I'm saying and
somehow align the two.

Wise words, beauty in strife,
small moments captured
in the hecticness of life.

II
Dog poo.

III
The Small Boy has
cried and
fussed and
refused to leave my side.
I strapped him on and wore him until
my back muscles cried with him, working
in the warmth of a pre-spring afternoon,
sunshine gilding his hair, like
yellow Labrador hair, and
the smiling eyes of our dogs.

I moved, and
used my body
the way it was designed, and
carrying a child so close felt like the small
Heaven of quiet-soul moments,
the sunbright warmth of
connected people, like
happy dog fur, which is both
happy-dog fur, and
happy dog-fur,
tumbling-freewheeling-spiralling in the breeze as I
scoop and shovel, scoop and shovel.

No one knew that dog poo could be spiritual.
(Well, possibly they did, but my soul had never heard it.)

IV
It's putting him to bed, forced
into slower rhythms
of twilit rooms, of
soft white humming, of
the washing machine and droning
from a far-distant TV.

It's knowing I can't leave because
he wants me close; it's realising that I
need him close.

When I have nothing better to do, I love
these night time rhythms.

I have nothing better to do.

V
I lie on the floor, still singing, still humming, and
for the first time all day
I relax, and
putting him to sleep is no longer hard work
draining work
but solace in a frantic day, and I
thank God for a small child who needs me,
even though I am tired of need,
because I need need, and he
needs me, and it because of this that
I am lying on the floor soothing
myself
as much as him.

VI
One day, I will remember these lessons
learned in soul-quiet moments.
The moments will run thicker—like
honey, maybe,
a sweet glaze over a life
well lived, slow
and luscious and dreamy.

## *WHEN WE KNOW BETTER*

One day, when I know you better,
I will peel back the
layers of my skin and
show you scars
time has long since healed:
perfect crescent moons
carved into aching flanks
by nails of regret.

One day, when you know me better,
you will learn
to read the language of these lines,
and you will know

That some days
these were the only words
I had to tell you:
Help me
I'm not coping
I'm not coping
I'm not coping

And some days,
they were crimson threads that bound me
to tangibility
when my head threatened to
sweep my feet from under
me.

One day, when we know each other better,
we will sit together
underneath
the stars of our achievements,
and we will see how
bright they shine,
and we will know
that stars are brighter than the crimson
lines we write upon our souls.

One day, when we both know better,
we will take a silver pen
and transcribe across our
souls the truth:
that we are precious
we are magic
we are kind

And the silver glow of our words
and the golden light of our stars
will outshine
all the crimson etchings of our guilt,
and we will rejoice.
For we are worth it.

## *NOTHING IS ENOUGH*

Sometimes,
you learn
that a pot of bubbling pasta
is enough.
When the seas of the world
wash over you,
when you crash upon the shores
of humanity's awful deeds,
when corporate greed,
poverty's dire need,
seek to drown you in their sorrow—

.stop.

We are not made to care
for the whole, wide world.

A pot of pasta bubbles beside me,
wholesome and natural and good,
homemade,
handmade,
devoid of the chemical taste of unchecked capitalism
a cruelty-free meal
for a world-weary soul.

Sometimes,
a pot of bubbling pasta
is enough.

## *WELTSCHMERZ*

The only thing I have
is hope.
(Please, don't scoff;
it's a fragile thing, I know.)
No magic bullet,
no empty promises,
no salves or balms for wounds
immeasurable.

But hope is what keeps us human.

(Destruction keeps us human, too,
and war, and self-annihilation;
offences on the climate, and
small, every-day atrocities,
committed without even thinking…
Humans, the living paradox: best
and worst
of the world, wrapped up in one neat package.)

A good thing, then, that hope
germinates in the dark.

A good thing, then, that hope
is viral,
a dandelion blooming into silver
and blown onwards by the breeze.

A good thing, then, that hope
burns brighter than the stars,
racing ever upward from its seed
though dirt,
through frost,
through rock and fire and rain,
seeking light,
shedding light.

Humans are equal parts
repository for darkness, and
collective vessel for hope.

So make a light for hope to find,
or if you can't, trust in the power of creative people
who can make those lights for others,
lights for hope to find,
lights for hope to grab on to;
and like that hope,
hold on.

And if you can't hold on,
hold me,
and I will drag you to the end.
I have no magic bullet,
no empty promises,
no salves or balms for wounds
immeasurable.
But together, we have hope.

## *WHAT DO I WANT YOU TO KNOW?*

I want you to know that
No matter how hard you try
There'll always be times when you fail
I want you to know that
No matter how many times you get back up to face the day,
Night will come again.
I want you to know that smiles don't erase tears,
that joy doesn't kill fears, that no matter how
big a person you are,
You will never, ever, ever have hands large
enough to carry the weight of the world.
I want you to know that you will watch
people you love suffer.
I want you to know that love
means hurting for another.
And I want you to know that you can scream and scream
and scream until
the dying of the light—
And some days nobody will hear you.

But I also want you to know
That no matter how many times you fail,
You can always rise up stronger.
I want you to know
That no matter how often comes the dark
Day will just as surely follow.
And on those Antarctic nights that seem to last
for months, not hours—count the stars.
Watch the beauty of the Southern
Lights as they play magic over your head,
vibrant, visible proof that your world is protected from on high.

I want you to know that even when the river of tears runs too deep for smiles,
even when the fears have you running for miles,
even when it seems as though the world will
crush you with its weight and break you with its wiles—
I love you.

Love means hurting for another.
And your hands will always be just that little bit too small.

But for now
for today
As we sit in a bathroom full of steam and you
stomp and clap and sing
Today your hand fits in mine, and
for you I can carry the weight of the world.
Today, I want you to know just one thing, and it is this:
Child: You are loved.

## *RECIPE FOR MY DAUGHTER*

Bright blonde curls and
Glimmering smile,
Shouting "I'm happy!"
(Or sometimes "I'm sad", but
More often than not it
Is 'happy')
So invested in everything you see
("It's scaring me."
"The goats, Daddy! The goats are
Not there! Oh no!")
So curious, determined
("The sun has gone! We have
To get it back.")
Fascination with your toes,
Dirt smudges on your chin,
(Or chocolate smears,
For every meal if
It were up to you.)

Living life hard and to the fullest,
Bikes and ballerinas,
Unicorns and umbrellas,
Dinosaurs and puppies,
You are as determined as the ageless mountains
And just as constant,
My homing-beacon,
Homebody, the way
back home when sands
Shift beneath my feet.
My compass, my lighthouse,
My mountain that stands watch over
The city of my life
While your arms
Are wrapped around me.

## *HERE IS MY BODY*

A pregnant woman's body is broken
For her children
In a way another's can never be,
Carrying her children for nine months
And nine months more
And nine months more
And nine months more,
Until all she can do is hold.
Our bodies are changed forever,
Stretch-marks and scars,
Feet broader or longer,
Hips wider, breasts larger,
Loose joints or back pain,
Gestational diabetes and RSI—
Not Tennis Elbow, Mother's Elbow.

Our bodies are broken down for them
Over
And over
And over
Again.

I can carry two giant bags of dog food all by myself,
Thanks, Mr Pet Store Man: I have mother's arms.

Can you carry the baby upstairs for me, husband?
My wrists are hurting and I can't face one more climb.

Broken and rebuilt, we are weakness, we are strength.
Here, child, is my body: broken for you.

## *RECIPE FOR MY SON*

Knobby knees
Brown-berry legs
(I remember when mine
Were like that too)
Dirt smears over your cheeks and
Glistening brown eyes and
Blond Harry Potter hair when it
Gets too long,
Gap-toothed smile and
Pride in your achievements,
Shirt painted with the tales of your day,
Living life full of passion,
My perpetual motion machine.

Never-ending questions,
Boundless enthusiasm,
Justice-sense honed like a knife,
Big, and loud, and bold, and unapologetic;
You are my humility, my patience,
My reminder of the vast, unexplored
expanses of the world,
The heart-buoying joy of discovery,
The sheer satisfaction gained through mastery,
The gradual accumulation of wisdom.
Your sister is a mountain, but
You, you are a tuning fork,
Vibrating to the hidden, constant rhythms
of the universe with delight.

## *STAND UP*

Sometimes,
When it feels like you are drowning,
All you need to do is stand.

Sometimes,
When it feels like land is far away,
It is really
Just under your feet.

It's amazing how panicked you can get
In three inches of water you weren't expecting.

## *LIMINAL SPACES*

Poetry
is a liminal space.
A moment of clarity, like
twelve-foot oceans where you see
a shape flashing beside you
in the water—bigger, smaller—
—bigger, smaller—only to realise
it's you,
it's your shadow,
skimming over the sand
dunes beneath the sea.

Poetry
is a liminal space,
an echoing hallway
designed to be occupied
by many; an epiphany that
applies to the masses
where the only occupant
is you.

Poetry
is liminal spaces,
the understandings in between,
the questions that slip sideways,
that flit between concrete ideas
like shadows, leaving behind nothing
but a shiver down your spine and
that fleeting feeling that something important
has just passed by.

Poetry
is a liminal space,
where the abstract, the unreal, borrows
the language of the concrete,
where thought becomes language becomes
writing on a page,
the essence of something true
distilled into something liquid,
something drinkable,
quicksilver for the soul.

Poetry
exists in the edges where, like
intertidal zones and ecotones, life
thrives as borders shift and change,
dynamic and alive with disturbance,
with fire—with drought.

Reading poetry
is like entering liminal spaces:
having left the tried and true,
we cross the threshold toward
understanding, unable yet to corral it
into tangible form.
What are we trying to say?
It doesn't matter, except to know that
our souls thrive in the edgelands,
the spaces borrowed for other purposes,
the long fluorescent hallways of the night.

Knowledge
is a brick, useful for building walls
or houses where our intellect resides;
but souls die for want of sunshine,
hearts wither for want of rain,
and it's in the liminal that things
collide—
like stars, like new life,
like inventions—
Like poems.

## *REMEMBER*

As you go through life,
remember to cast your nets behind you.
Trawl through the wreckage of broken dreams:
the diamonds and discarded pearls will snag in your nets
and when the empty-handed come to you,
broken, like their dreams,
you can spread your long-fingered grasp and say—
Here, these, this
is what I found amongst the rubble others threw away
This is what I gathered from the dust-encrusted
ankle-breaking
scraper-high stacks
of dreams that others left behind
This is what you find
when your nets are woven of starshine and hope
glimmering pieces of silver, refusing to give up, give in, or
                                        give out.

## *ABOUT THE AUTHOR*

AMY LAURENS wishes she were a better poet than she is. Words are so frustratingly *heavy* for some of life's more intangible moments. Still, she's better at words than, say, interpretive dance, so she'll make do with the ones she has.

Amy has also published numerous books full of words,* including several fantasy novels for children and some more for adults, some non-fiction for writers, some non-fiction for people who are alive, and a bunch of random short stories. You can find them at www.amylaurens.com/books. (Though her blog at www.amylaurens.com is probably the best place to find things similar in tone to these poems—search for the tags 'learning to run', 'if only you knew', 'restoration of my soul' or 'throwing starfish', or look for the category 'truly, madly deeply'.)

* Okay, one of the books of short stories has pictures in it that she drew too.

www.ingramcontent.com/pod-product-compliance
Lightning Source LLC
Chambersburg PA
CBHW071317080526
44587CB00018B/3260